Trucks
Byron Barton

A TRUMPET CLUB SPECIAL EDITION

Published by The Trumpet Club
666 Fifth Avenue, New York, New York 10103
Copyright © 1986 by Byron Barton.   All rights reserved.
This edition published by arrangement with HarperCollins Publishers.
Printed in the United States of America.   October 1992.
ISBN 0-440-84993-4   DAN   10 9 8 7 6 5 4 3 2 1

On the road

here come the trucks.

They come through tunnels.

They go over the bridge.

Here comes the bread truck

with bread for the store.

Here is a truck being loaded

with garbage.

Here comes a truck

bringing the newspapers.

Here is a bucket truck

to help fix the lights.

This is a tank truck

delivering oil.

Here comes a tow truck towing a car.

Here is a moving truck

bringing the furniture.

This truck brings hot dogs

and ice cream and soda.

Here is a dump truck

hauling dirt.

This is a cement truck

mixing cement.

Here is a truck working all night long.

Trucks on the road. They work hard.